BLEEDING FLOWERS

A Collection of Poetry

B|eeding F|owers

A Collection of Poetry

Shay Siegel

BLEEDING FLOWERS. Copyright © 2019 by Shay Siegel. All rights reserved. No part of this book may be used or reproduced in any manner whatsoever without written permission from the author, except in the case of brief quotations.

FIRST EDITION, 2019
Printed in the United States of America

Cover Design by Dominick Neuner

ISBN: 978-0-578-51679-0

www.shaysiegel.com

Table of Contents

Bleeding Flowers 1
Only Thing to Do 2
When Ripped Apart 3
Two as One 4
We Were Who We Were 5
Plastic 6
Do You Suffocate, Too? 7
Life Without Parole 8
Memory Box 9
Ghosts of Memories 10
She Said 11
Sweet Lies 12
The Friendship Necklace 13
Conditional Love 15
You Should Feel It, Too 17
The Before Picture Was Better 18
The Eye 19
Illusions 20
Was 21
You Weren't There 22
Rib-Caged 23

Slowly	24
One	26
Roots	27
HIM	28
I Hear You Loudly	29
Heart Ache	30
Soundless Scream	31
Hidden	32
Within Her	34
Don't	36
If Only	37
Red Drops	38
Alive in Blood	39
Dirt	40
The Flower Grew	41
Frosted	42
Avalanche	43
Winter, You Are Cold	44
Fireplace	45
Moon Sky	46
Whistle	48
The Storm	49
Dreaming for You	50

The Moment	51
Inside the Cellar	53
Sundial	54
Lost in the Fog	55
Is There More?	56
See	57
Ruthless Waves	58
Belonging to Sea	59
Sandcastle	60
Fighting for Air	61
The Ocean is Where my Heart is	62
Cultivation	63
Crushed Flowers	64
The Red Sweater	65
The Pen is Mightier	66
Galaxy of Dreams	67
Tree House in the Woods	68
I Love You	70
All Withers Again	72
Acknowledgements	73
About the Author	74

Bleeding Flowers

My heart is a grave
in the cold ground.
Flowers have grown upon it
despite its frozen darkness,
and their petals bleed
for all that lies inside.

Shay Siegel

Only Thing to Do

What feels
like the most complicated
thing to do
was the only
thing we had to do
when we entered this world
...breathe.

When Ripped Apart

Rending through the body,
demanding to be lived.

It has no inkling
of why,
or what it wants,
only to take a breath.

Would it force its path
if it knew every
disappointment that lingered
on the other side of this womb?

Would it request
to be here
if it understood
the festering heart sores
that would one day decorate it
like daisies in a field?
Blooming, blossoming
Wilting
Dying

Once, life was only
about entering the world
with no views,
expectations,
hopes,
or anything other
than breathing.

Shay Siegel

Two as One

Some used to envy
our friendship.
They couldn't understand
two humans so in tune.

They'd say, it's fascinating,
best friends
who don't remember meeting.

Because we met when
memories weren't likely to form,
sharing a crib,
and blankets,
stuffed toys, and warm skin.

Infants, placed together,
only breathing
side by side.

So it's no wonder
that my lungs
feel flatter now.

My heart beats
just a little slower,
and oxygen doesn't fill me.

How could I be good at breathing
when I learned how to do it
with the one person
who made me want to stop?

We Were Who We Were

It was 1990 when we met,
before we were who we were.

The nineties were running through sprinklers
in summer,
playing whiffle ball in the yard,
popsicles,
make-believe games, stick horses,
and dances to Green Day.

The 2000s were much the same,
with crushes, dear diaries,
womanhood, and makeup
sprinkled about like the dandelion seeds
we used to blow into the sun.

By 2014, you ripped me
from your life
like a page of paper
in a Lisa Frank notebook
we wrote songs and dreams in.

And here I am,
floating on the breeze,
waiting to land somewhere
far away
from my own mind
where your memory
lives in so many
different colors.

Plastic

One day, your plastic shell
will fall from you,
and with nothing left
to hide beneath,
you'll ache like I do.

Do You Suffocate, Too?

When loneliness
presses the breath
out of your chest,
do you think of me?

Or is suffocating better
than admitting
your regret?

Shay Siegel

Life Without Parole

You were the one
who slaughtered us.
So why am I
serving your life sentence?

Memory Box

When we were young,
we buried a memory box
full of objects important to us.

I wish we never dug it up.
Maybe, then, the recollections
could stay in their tomb.

Now, they sit in the open
just as they did
when we uncovered the sodden box,
and found letters to our future selves
disintegrated,
your horse statue's leg
broken by the weather,
my tennis ball
muddied with rain.

Did you know that *us* was important to me, too?
Maybe it would all be better
if it had just stayed buried.

Shay Siegel

Ghosts of Memories

Why is it that forgetting
is so easy
when there's no threat
of the forgotten
haunting us forever?

She Said

She told me,
"I think my dad
is proud of me."

She once mentioned
that no matter
what I did
she would stand behind me.

She said,
"You could kill someone
and I'd think
the world was better off."

She talked about
how we were the same.

She talked
She told me
She mentioned
I listened

She said, she said, she said
Lies.

Sweet Lies

You wrapped your lies
in rose petals
that smelled sweet
and were silky to touch,

but flowers can't live
forever.
You knew they'd shrivel,
losing their vibrancy,
and I'd
glimpse the truth

after everything
had already
wilted.

The Friendship Necklace

A heart broken in half,
jagged and uneven,
dangling from a cheap,
itchy chain—
the type that turns your flesh green.

Fake metal masquerading
as something valuable.
Something meaningful.

Until, one day, it breaks,
or maybe you lose it.
You lie to yourself,
saying how much
it meant to you.

Even if you
don't know yet
that it was doomed
to be nothing.

It's gone in a hiss of wind,
you never noticed it go.

Eventually, you forget.
You replace it with a new chain—
something better—
and your neck won't be alone
anymore.

Shay Siegel

You grow up.
You only wear platinum,
or silver,
or diamonds now.

You remember what was,
and how foolish those
Broken
Hearts
Were.

Because everything has an end.

Conditional Love

You said you loved me,
but lied.

You said I was your sister,
blood or not.

You let me give your son
a name.

It means the Lord is gracious,
you are not.

You plucked me
from his life

like a dandelion
in a field of thousands.

And that wasn't all,
though perhaps the worst.

You were my sister,
blood or not.

You made me laugh,
but why did you hate me?

I gave you my childhood.
You gave me heartbreak.

Shay Siegel

You were not
what I thought,

no one
did.

I forgive,
because it's all that's left.

You are not my sister,
blood or not.

My love was conditional
after it all.

You Should Feel It, Too

I wish I could say I understood.
I've spent my life trying,
spilling my humanity from
every vein,
every breath,
every teardrop.

But my mind will not stand
for the trying.
It will not grasp
what you've done,
and though my beating heart has tried
on its own,
it only wants for you to feel
the agony
you've drowned me in.

It wants you to throb
in the same way I do.

Shay Siegel

The Before Picture Was Better

You were before.
I don't know what after
looks like.
I'm not sure I want to.

The Eye
A Haiku

Watch how it can lie
It deceives from the inside
Betrayal hidden

Shay Siegel

Illusions

What I liked about you
was that you were
a friend,
made me complete,
and we existed together.

Only,
I was not whole,
was not living,
and was as alone as the heart
in my chest.

I see that now,
but I don't know
if I can trust my eyes anymore.

Was

I miss what was
because what I was
I never can be again

Shay Siegel

You Weren't There

There are moments where
I don't care
that you flicked me aside
like dust

because we shared a crib, a bed,
secrets in the backyard tent,
and it all dissolved
like colored sprinkles in hot water.

Couldn't we pretend you were good,
like the make-believe games we used to play?
Just for a short while,
so you could bandage my wounds
and tell me I was worthy.

Maybe I could forget
they were
poisonous hands holding me
in the dark.

I still wish you were here
to sit in the somber with me,
our hearts listening for each other,
because how much can one heart
sustain alone?

Rib-Caged

My heart lives inside a cage
trapped in blackness
beating for no one to hear.

Maybe it was made for this;
it would expire in the light.

Slowly

It happened slowly
like spilled coffee
pooling into the copse,
rotting from the surface
first,
as it spread across
inching and dripping
toward the edges,

forming silhouettes
and shadows,
morphing and changing
the longer it lingered.

It happened slowly
like that,
when one depleted moment
turned into thousands,
drifting into the calm
before finding the storm
each time.

Shifting and swimming,
rotting from the surface
until it reached
the inside
and ate away
at the workings
of what kept it
intact,
drowning for no one to see.

Bleeding Flowers

It happens slowly like that.

One

We spent each breath
entwined,
no thoughts our own.

Everything muddled,
mixed up in a pot,
boiling,
spilling,

we were one.

One person
desperately needing to
detach.

Roots

Sometimes
my heart still believes
that the seeds you planted within it
will blossom into flowers.

Deep down,
like roots in soil,
it knows you poisoned them.
No way to bloom,
only to wait in bleeding darkness
forever.

HIM

You
make me wonder
if He looks down
upon the contagion
bleeding from your fingertips,
and maybe He thinks
He was wrong
to sacrifice.

I Hear You Loudly

Even when I can't hear you,
you thud against my ears
with a viciousness
I cannot mute.

My heart burns
from the middle
to the edges
when I think of you.

And sometimes I wonder
if one single memory
wields all the strength it needs
to erase me.

Heart Ache

I hear you
reaching inside
with barbed fingers,
closing on my heart

pulling and pulling
until you drag it through
bones
and sinews,
the inside of flesh

when
it connects with the air
and stops.

I hear you slaying me
from within
the abyss,
until I can't hear
anything
but blackness.

Soundless Scream

I feel you as much as the shadow
stirring along the floor
when he enters my mind
and seals it with
doubts.

I hear you as much as the silhouette
slinking silently.

Not one creak in the wood,
but he scrapes against my brain,
pulsating
loudly.

My breath holds still.
I forget to let the air out
or in.

He paces on my chest
with feet viscous and deliberate.

I feel you,
pressing existence out
through the seams of my skin.

Hidden

Garnet spreads
through ivory cloth,
shaping a single flower.

A knife rests
beside her
on the floor.

Red droplets
caressing the metal
like summer rain.

Some have drizzled
the carpet,
but it's black.

They go unnoticed
to everyone
except her.

The fabric soaks up
desolation
until it's crusted and dry.

She sweeps her face,
but the shame
can't be wiped away.

She runs her raw wound
under a cold
quieting stream of water.

Bleeding Flowers

Other white and pink scars
adorn her arm like
pastel paint,

some more luminous
than others.
Variant broken canvas.

She pats dry,
throws the bleeding towel
away,

puts on a smile
that hides the blood
and sharp objects,

the same way
her jacket, stitched with red roses,
does.

Within Her

Hurt
blooms between her thighs,
a reminder of where you were

when she drank until
the edges of the world
turned black,

until her throat burned sour
and she wanted to bleed
into puddles of extinction.

She's done it before,
she will again.

Not with you,
someone who is the same.

Who doesn't notice
how charred she is inside

when she removes layers,
illuminating thrashes
of raised skin
down her legs,

each scar possessing memories
of what's gone bad.
A life unlived
or lived too much.

Bleeding Flowers

It doesn't matter,
she's already dissolving
from the outside in.

Don't

Please stop,
it hurts—the way
you've hollowed my soul.

Take the noose
from my
heart.

It can't breathe,
but I guess
that's okay.

I don't
recognize
this life,

my organs
don't crave
the ozone anyway.

If Only

She gazes the horizon,
jagged cliffs of moss and rocks.
So inviting—putrid.

But she's inside. Alone.
Always alone
in the uncomfortable comfort.

If she just had the resolution
to walk
out the front door.

She could glide upon the cliff's edge,
look down at the water crashing
onto harsh, glassy rocks.

She could perish, a striking fatality,
slipping from the burden,
into the nothingness of water.

Dark streams of red,
morphing with
blue liquid.

Peace flooding through her,
like crimson
engulfing the ocean.

How exquisite,
how tragic and serene,
soaring into silence.

Red Drops

Red drops
Red drops of blood

Dripping from her blade
Her caustic blade

Scars on her arm
Her addled arm

Teardrops
Teardrops of blood

Sliding down her face
Her dismal face

Scars on her heart
Her severed heart

Crimson smears the floor
The strong floor

Exhale the ugly drippings
Such ugly drippings

Red drops
Red drops are peace

Alive in Blood

Sometimes I need to see
my red blood
from the outside
to know that it exists.

Dirt

She lived her whole life
killing herself
to be a flower.

Every day, watering,
preening,
whispering courage.
Only to be battered by winter
before she could blossom.

And as she sat in the blue cold,
she realized
she had been bleeding
and bleeding
for the dirt.

The Flower Grew

She looked down
from the clouds
at her body
lying in a field of wildflowers.

They sprouted in shades
of blue,
indigo,
blush, and sunshine

from her veins,
her spine, and heart,
and she felt
she was finally beautiful.

Frosted

Frost bit her
through the surface layer
of skin,

piercing
the capillaries
with pinschers
of ice.

She said, *it'll heal*

but the scar tissue
will remember.

Avalanche

A wound
isn't so bad
when it's done
spilling from the vein

like the slow slide of
an avalanche,
it fuses together
and becomes a distant
casualty.

Unless lingering,
digging at the edges,
it breaks
from the outside in,
splitting open—a drink of sleet
through the mouth of a cave.

Let the blood dry beneath
sunrays
and melt the snow.

Shay Siegel

Winter, You Are Cold

Crisp, glacial air
hands meet pockets
chills scatter shoulder blades
Winter, you are cold

Puddles on the sidewalk
ready to freeze over
I see blooming tulips ahead
but only feel winter

Bursts of wind
whirling, whistling at the air
crunchy leaves fluttering
through the heavy day

Ice chips in my veins
under gray striped skies
numbness takes over
Winter, you are cold

Put me back inside
place me by the fire
the tulips do not live here
Winter, you are cold

Fireplace

I want to crawl inside the fireplace,
smolder in the ashes,
reborn

I want to burn my flesh,
glow orange,
brighter

I want my bones to melt,
take a break from the
snow

I want veils of smoke
swirling through my
veins

I want to feel the hurt
from the outside
in

Like a hot cup of tea
seeping through my
viscera

Let the fire consume me
because I'm nothing in the
cold

Moon Sky

Once, I looked at the moon,
a missing sliver
remained in shadow,
not glowing with the rest
of what it was part of.

I looked at the orb
against the black
backdrop of sky,
taking so much space
but too far away
to touch.

It shined
for no one
and everyone.

I envied it,
not caring
about the world
and its opinions,
as it soaked up awe
and went
ignored.

It would be beautiful
to have one sliver
missing,
and not the
whole center
of my heart

Bleeding Flowers

in shadow.

Whistle

Teach me how to whistle
like the skirl of the wind

one you feel sting your body
during a whiteout

the crackle of the fireplace
sparking and bursting

but the whistle invades the chimney
lurid and known

it cannot be ignored
despite its invisibility

an entity existing
no one can debate

teach me how to be heard
how to live in the open

like a whistle of wind
saying,
I'm here.

The Storm

Night seeps in,
oozing indigo and gray,
thunder smashes through the wind
shouting regrets,
raining blame,
and lightning strikes
of truth.

A storm we can't ignore,
but we wait for its end.

Dreaming for You

If I knew you'd slip
into my dreams
each night,
I'd stay asleep forever.

Then, I wouldn't
crumble beneath the strength
of reality
...that you aren't here.

The Moment

I want to live in the moment
between awake and asleep

nestle my cheek in satin,
paralyzed

hair twisted against temple
eyes slouching, jaw slithering away

drivel seeping into fibers
against cracked lips

travel to times made up of dreams
that aren't real

silk sheets slide beneath me
as I lay still

transcending,
take a trip without moving

there is no tomorrow,
only right now, as I wilt into the void

electrocuted with brilliance,
forgotten in morning

changing the world doesn't matter,
only weighted eyelids and calm

Shay Siegel

nothing as important
as cocooning in cotton

burrowed
with a leg sticking out

breathing echoed and slow,
brain numb

fatality in fingertips
and moonlight on face

I want to feel it all
until I can no longer feel anything

between feeling and not feeling
where the world makes sense and doesn't

I want to live in the moment between awake and asleep
the moment whole lives are lived in

Inside the Cellar

It is empty
but safe

It is cramped
and dim

It is static
just fine

No need
to see beyond
the cellar door.

Sundial

The radiator
hums in the bedroom
sunlight has not
favored the yard
time passes and we wait

Olive grass
through the panes of time
bright rays have not
delivered themselves upon
the untouched land

Rusty sundial
cold in the ground
no shine, no shadows
rendered useless
when time stands still

This dusty room
desolate and morose
clock on the wall
ticking and waiting
for what is missing

Lost in the Fog

In the woods,
there is only
the fog
to kiss
my skin
with lips tender
and invisible.

Tree trunks stand tall
even when the fierce
gusts
try to crack them.

Another unseen force,
but depraved,
and testing their insides,
which are stronger than mine.

Is There More?

Ever stare at the faultless sky,
feel the breeze on your face,
wonder why life's fleeting by,
if it's all a waste?

Listen for the rhythm of birds,
smell the dew of grass,
wonder if you'll be heard,
why existence is crass?

Jump in the silky, silent bay,
taste salt on your lips,
wonder if there's more to say
about the emptiness....

See

Seagrass swaying
Springtime fraying
Waves crashing
Sand thrashing

Skies clouding
Sun drowning
Storms brewing
Night birds cooing

Rain pelting
Daytime melting
Star-speckled night
Mutilated light

Dawn breaking
Sun waking
Moving ahead
It's all been said

Ruthless Waves

I live in an ocean
full of regret,
crashing down on me
with the vigor
of waves on the shore.

Saltwater should heal,
it is home,
but my haven
is way out
drowning.

Belonging to Sea

Where sand sticks to sweat
and cold water paralyzes
my heart glides out to sea
drifting under the sun

my soul cycles the waves
until sucked underneath
pulled into the tide's floor
where it belongs

Shay Siegel

Sandcastle

I mold a sandcastle on the beach
open the door and wither

Waves burst around me
roaring in my ears

Sea glass, weathered and worn,
scatters pink toes

Piping plovers nest beyond
safe in grassy dunes

Gulls wave at the clouds
squawking a melody of searching

Salt drifts on the breeze
healing bones and sadness

I'll sit in my sandcastle by the shore
and watch my life float out to sea

Fighting for Air

I was
trapped below
the surface of
water.

I saw the light
but couldn't
reach out
and feel
air.

I've swam now
up
and up.

And as my skull
broke through the tide,
I took a breath
like I'd die if I didn't.

Shay Siegel

The Ocean is Where my Heart is

Breathing comes
easier
beside the ocean.

Salt water
is home,
healing,
and clarity.

It is the lungful
of air
that has
always meant
everything
will be okay.

Cultivation

Plucking a flower
from a garden
takes one moment,

but allowing it to grow
into what it could be
takes blood

entrenched in soil,
traveling through stems
and petals,
like winding veins,

sent up
and into the light.

Shay Siegel

Crushed Flowers

She held the crushed flowers
in her hands
and realized the beauty was in
the sweet fragrance

The Red Sweater

The red sweater
hung in the closet,
cramped beside
every other
layer.

I took it down,
remembering
the feel of cotton and fun
at Christmas dinner
and in the February cold.

But, that turned into
wearing it alone
where it'd catch the tears
in its fibers.

It doesn't look
like it did then.
It's faded,
fits wrong,
the fabric scratchy.

The color used to
hide the blood,
when I needed it to,
but I don't bleed anymore.

Winter has passed.
I toss it into the pile
of what I no longer need.

The Pen is Mightier

When you deleted me
I did not rewrite myself.

But, now, as I sit
staring out
at rustling maple leaves
and blooming daffodils,

I touch pen
to paper.

Galaxy of Dreams

We built a tree house
that we called
Galaxy of Dreams

with rusted nails
and broken planks
of wood,
frayed cords,
and plastic.

I'll create a
tree house
on my own,
one that
withstands the weather

because my dreams
are a galaxy
all by themselves.

Shay Siegel

Tree House in the Woods

I'd like to live in a tree house in the woods
inhale the secrets whispered by the wind
and share my solitude
with wild turkeys and deer

I'd like to neighbor beside a family of squirrels
whisper my own secrets into the depths of the wind
and tell the blue jay that his coat
reminds me of ink-splashed quills

I'd like to feel the itch of bark and fire ants on my skin
pull someone else's secrets from the wind
if I stretch my ear to the swath of clouds
and listen hard enough

I'd like to follow maple leaves as they dance and break away
breathe the nectar of morning dew and pine-cedar air
focus on the buzzing of the bumblebee
when the wind stands still

I'd like to watch pinecones scatter the earth like droplets of rain
while my feet remain planted in the watercolor sky
the wind returns with a secret kiss, rustling hair against my ears,
a whisper slipping through my skin

I'd like to live in a tree house in the woods
where secrets bloom then fall away in the wind
drifting down to the ground like dandelion petals

Bleeding Flowers

where I can shut my eyes beneath windows carved in oak
melt my flesh with the sun
nestled like a humming bird in a rose...safe and free.

I Love You

All who cross
each season
of my life
I love.

The woman who took
and took,
the girl who was everything,
but dropped,
the lady who abused.

I love those
who crowded my brain
and heart
with
doubts
fears
hatred
and jealousy.

The ones who could not
construct time,
who didn't bother
to ask questions
or care for
the burden of answers.

The ones who don't see
the bleeding flowers
growing from my skin.

Bleeding Flowers

I will love and hate you
at once.
My soul
wants it that way.

It will be
from a distance.
Abandoned, but not extinct.

You regarded me
with apathy
so my love can
no longer breathe for you.

Though sometimes it aches
to admit
the love exists
because I am
human.

All Withers Again

I think,
perhaps,
I may appreciate
the beauty of
an iris
under the halo of the sun,
with the knowledge
that winter dawns again.

Acknowledgements

First, I would like to thank *you*, the readers. Your connection with my work means everything.
I'd like to thank those who played a role in helping me develop my craft, and encouraging me to keep writing, especially at Tulane University and Sarah Lawrence College.
My family has always supported me in my writing pursuits and I truly cherish that. Mom and Dad, thank you. Thank you to my sister, Jen, and my brother-in-law, Mike, for always listening. Thank you to my friend, Dominick, for working so hard on this beautiful cover.
Thank you to Pat, who may not understand my writing and what goes on inside my head (which is possibly for the best) but always supports me, nonetheless.

About the Author

Shay Siegel is from Long Island, New York. She graduated from Tulane University with a B.A. in English, where she was also a member of the women's tennis team. She went on to earn an MFA in Writing from Sarah Lawrence College. She currently lives in Columbia, South Carolina with her boyfriend, Pat, and their giant-headed shelter pup, Bernie.

Website: www.shaysiegel.com
Instagram: @shaysiegelauthor
Facebook: @shaysiegelwriter

www.ingramcontent.com/pod-product-compliance
Lightning Source LLC
Chambersburg PA
CBHW021959290426
44108CB00012B/1132